"CAPTAIN THUNDERBOLT"

FREDERICK WORDSWORTH WARD

"THE AUSTRALIAN BUSHRANGER"

Colin Teasdale

FREDERICK WORDSWORTH WARD
"CAPTAIN THUNDERBOLT"
'THE AUSTRALIAN BUSHRANGER'

First published in Australia by Colin Teasdale 2025

A catalogue record for this
book is available from the
National Library of Australia

ISBN: 978-0-6482243-9-6 (hardback)

Typesetting and design by Publicious Book Publishing
Published in collaboration with Publicious Book
Publishing. www.publicious.com.au

Cover image: Margo Harrison © Shutterstock
crown image: Tartila © Shutterstock

Dedications:

H.R.H

E^{II}R

To Her Royal Highness - Her Majesty, Queen
Elizabeth - II, Queen of England, your Spirit will reign
with your compassion, admiration, loyalty, love and
kindness, over England and the World eternally.
GOD BLESS YOU!
Colin Teasdale 20/5/2023

And

For Frederick Wordsworth Ward with his faithful
companion "The Steed". He rode the plains, the hills
and valleys that surrounded him. Fred Ward lived his
life a tormented soul, leading a nomadic existence
to explore a new boundary within. He became
Australia's finest Bushranger!

The man, "Thunderbolt", walks on the plains, in the distance with his chestnut-coloured horse. He wears his cowboy hat and holds his horse with a long rein behind him. You can see him walking into the horizon, with his head bowed, and a beautiful sunset in the background.

He is The Australian Bushranger!

FREDERICK WORDSWORTH WARD "CAPTAIN THUNDERBOLT"

I bring forth to you a legend, a man that has been forgotten and lost in time. The man, a cowboy, but a bushranger! The "Thoroughbred"—"Steed". The "Ship". The land of the "country,"—'his'—"ocean". His name, "Thunderbolt"—"Captain Thunderbolt"—The name he inherited and was branded with by the citizens he unfortunately robbed.

In 1835, Frederick Wordsworth Ward was born just outside Sydney NSW, near the Hawkesbury River. He is believed to have died on 25 May 1870. Rumour has it he was shot by a constable at Kentucky Creek, in rough terrain near Church Gully, Uralla. Speculation is, as suggested by historians, that the person buried at Uralla Cemetery NSW was not Ward, and that some other person had taken his place. Ward's death is said to have had no credibility in that it was actually him who was buried at the grave site.

It remains a mystery. The tale of "Captain Thunderbolt" has eluded everyone to this day. Over the 6½ years of spree, Ward robbed anybody who had gold on them (or not). Apparently, he had a lust for the 'precious yellow metal' and he hoarded every taking he got hold of. He used his prizes as his personal collection to admire for himself. He would then hide it or, most of all, bury it in the ground where he could find it again. He would create a marker so he could easily locate it.

When it came to his gold takings, when desired, he would make sure that the gold hoards were in the safest place possible. He could then be at ease and when he had the desire, he could go to where he buried or hid his gold relics, close to his hideout. From what is known, he liked caves, mainly for his hideouts, but also so he could recuperate and rest after his ordeals and escapades on his trails. There were main caves, and Ward's takings in gold were either buried or hidden as close to his domain as possible, knowing it would be safe and free from being seen so the hoards of gold could not be taken by marauders. "Captain Thunderbolt" robbed! He robbed mailmen, travellers, inns, stores, coaches, prospectors, and anybody who was carrying, storing and dealing in gold. The list of his takings would include gold jewellery, gold chains, gold watches, gold bullion, gold sovereigns, gold coins, and any other gold items that were valuable.

As legend tells, he was known to have had bags of gold and sovereign coins loaded on his horse, which happened to be a thoroughbred steed always ready to ride like the wind back to his place of rest. Then, when back at his domain, he would lust over his takings and when satisfied, he would bury or hide it.

There is no evidence to suggest that Ward ever shot anyone (or at anyone) on his escapades when he took his pay loads in gold from the people he had robbed. He was known to show his pistols, but rather than discharging them, he would bluff the people into handing over their precious property. There is no mention of any bank robberies. Very little evidence exists and suggests that this was not the case.

Ward apparently stole a horse, but it is said that the horse that was in his possession escaped and had broken out of a country property, thus resulting in him being branded a thief. Ward, or "Captain Thunderbolt", gained his nickname through robberies he committed. Witnesses had said that when Ward came through the doors of the premises he was going to rob, he sounded like a thunderbolt, thus inheriting the nickname—"Captain Thunderbolt". This name is known to this day.

Speculated evidence says that Ward did not die during a shoot-out at Kentucky Creek when police were said to have shot him dead on 25 May 1870. I have mentioned this before in this biography in which I have written about this forgotten and lost soul.

A man, a "cowboy", a bushranger. His "Steed", "The Ship", the land of the country, his ocean. "Captain Thunderbolt" and his legacy lives on. There not a lot of knowledge and information about "Thunderbolt". The life he led was very much secluded.

Not much was known about him and his ventures. His trail routes were Gloucester to Inverell in New South Wales. One of his original routes and trails was between Hunter Valley and the North West Slopes and Plains. Captain Thunderbolt's trails also ran through the Barrington Tops State Forest. These trails are extremely hard to access as they are in very rough terrain. To find the complex network of trails he formed is difficult as he was the only one who knew where the trails were. There is also dense scrub in this area, which is impenetrable.

Thunderbolts Way leads from Armidale in New South Wales to the vicinity of Bundarra, Uralla and Kentucky in New South Wales. "Captain Thunderbolt's" main cave is also located there. This cave he vacated would have been his abode, his permanent place of rest and peace. This cave would have been his home. There he would eat, sleep and recuperate himself from the worry of being captured. The only thing he would have cared about at this abode would have been his beloved, faithful thoroughbred steed to whom he cherished. The only thing he could rely on that would not let him down—The "Thoroughbred"—"Steed" "The Ship". All his gold hoards would be in safe places—at his home, everywhere, always close by for easy access and for him to locate for himself. He could also very well have hidden and buried his takings in crevices, having special markers to lead him to where his hoards were. You would just have to put your mind in his mind to decide what you would do as "Captain Thunderbolt". You would basically do the same things when it came to where to stash your gold takings. You would obviously bury it and hide the takings in the safest place possible. The closest spots to keep it safe would be as close to his hideouts as possible so he couldn't be captured, and to eliminate the fear of being caught somewhere on his trails with his horse. If it was me, I would put the gold takings as close to my hideout as I could so I wouldn't be seen or captured. I would, at leisure, go to the area where I had stashed my takings, just to appreciate and admire the gold I had.

Six and a half years of more and more consuming and hoarding. His obsession with having gold inspired him. It would have thrilled him to just look at his treasures. But if I was him, I would hide my loot as close as I possibly could to my hideout. I would not have any fear or worry about getting captured or caught. But the question is: Where did Ward, or "Captain Thunderbolt" put his treasures?

If he in fact didn't get killed in 1870, he was a free man and lived his life as a nomad. The isolation, I suppose, he would have overcome. He was 'free' to live his life never too be heard of again. But the mystery remains—where did he venture? Where did he live his life after being a bushranger, who rode a thoroughbred steed as his ship that crossed the ocean? He had shown his pistols without discharging them or using them on anyone—without hurting any person or citizen. This in itself is extraordinary. When he robbed citizens of their precious possessions, it was all their gold. The feeling must have been overwhelming for him when this was happening, "knowing" he had the "Thoroughbred"—"Steed". The "Ship" on standby, ready to ride like the wind, to carry him back to his lair, his hideout, his home. The Faithful"—"Steed". The "Ship". The freedom of knowing what he had achieved was over once again, and he was on his way back to his abode. He would have to then recuperate and replenish himself, but also attend to his "beloved"— "Thoroughbred"—"Steed Express."—The "Ship", of "Freedom", "Glory", and "Destiny".

"Fred Ward" is "renowned" as a "great"— "master"—"horseman", he also had hideouts and trails all around the New England area in

New South Wales as he would have favoured being as close to his main hideout as possible. A cave to bury his hoards of gold takings. This would have been his main objective to stop himself from riding long distances away from his main abode. This would have been a precautionary measure to not jeopardise himself and risk being seen or captured when he rode to his secret locations. If he were to bury his gold takings along desolate trails, the fear would be with him that he would be captured or seen. What would I do if I was a bushranger? I would stay at a main hideout where all my gold hoards were buried and hidden, so I would stop venturing away and riding long distances.

If I had buried my takings on trails a long way away from my main abode, I would be in constant fear of being captured. So, I would think it would be a very wise decision to bury or hide the loot as close to the main hideout as possible. I would take what I needed in money, enough to purchase goods to survive from.

With this book, I endeavour to make "Captain Thunderbolt's" name famous and put his name in Australian folklore and manuscript history. He, "Captain Thunderbolt," has been totally forgotten and abandoned. An Australian bushranger, Frederick Wordsworth Ward, aka "Captain Thunderbolt's" name should be put in archival institutions all over Australia. He is Australia's greatest bushranger ever. Remembering that he never shot anyone, or at anyone, when he planned to rob them of their precious possessions. Witnesses verified this at the time of the incidents. It is sad to think, and comprehend, that someone else took his place in archival history as Australia's legendary bushranger.

It is also hard to imagine that he had an imposter. It is a very sad state of affairs that someone like Frederick Wordsworth Ward—"Captain Thunderbolt"—could ever be left out of the archival folklore history as a legendary Australian bushranger. Another person has taken his place.

I also think it is extremely unfair to not recognise the fact that Ward was forgotten and lost in time. It is very unfortunate to this day! How could his name disappear and not be famously recognised as the most legendary bushranger Australia has ever had? Ward, or "Captain Thunderbolt" as he was known, succeeded in his endeavours and escapades, which was to carry out the most daring and calculated robberies of all time. And this was done without bringing any harm to the people he robbed of their possessions. He got away with the lot. In Australian folklore history of

Australian bushrangers, Ward, or "Captain Thunderbolt," has been excluded and ignored as one of the greatest bushrangers Australia has ever had. The other bushranger was made a legend instead of "Captain Thunderbolt". Being known as the individual, "Captain Thunderbolt," or "The Cowboy", is one thing, but a bushranger means his name is more appropriate than the other imposter. The other imposter was made legendary and famous in Australian folklore history instead of Ward, or "Captain Thunderbolt". This is how folklore history has prevailed, and I believe "Captain Thunderbolt" should have been recognised instead of the other imposter that exists today and was made famous instead.

There is a statue of Ward, or "Captain Thunderbolt", on his beloved "Steed" at the crossroad of New England Highway and Thunderbolts Way, Uralla in New South

Wales. Uralla, New South Wales is also supposed to have the burial site and grave of "Captain Thunderbolt". This is where he was supposedly laid to rest.

The man, a cowboy, but a bushranger. His "Thoroughbred"—"Steed",—His "Ship." The land of the "country," his, "ocean". His name, "Captain Thunderbolt", reigns on. The "beloved," "Thoroughbred"—"Steed",—The "Ship", who had been so "faithful" to him, is not forgotten. His spirit will reign forever in time. And his name will go down as one of the greatest bushrangers Australia has ever had.

The story ends here. He walked into the oblivion with his "beloved," "Steed," The "Horse", vanishing into the wilderness, never to be seen or heard of again.

Fact remains, nobody really knows what happened to Fred Ward, "Captain Thunderbolt", and his companion.

The subject remains bewildering, and it will mystify us through time. He achieved nothing in his life that was good. Gold hoards, were secretly hidden, never to be found, citizens got hurt. The spirit of Fred Ward will continue to linger on in people's minds as he walked on to redemption.

C.B.T

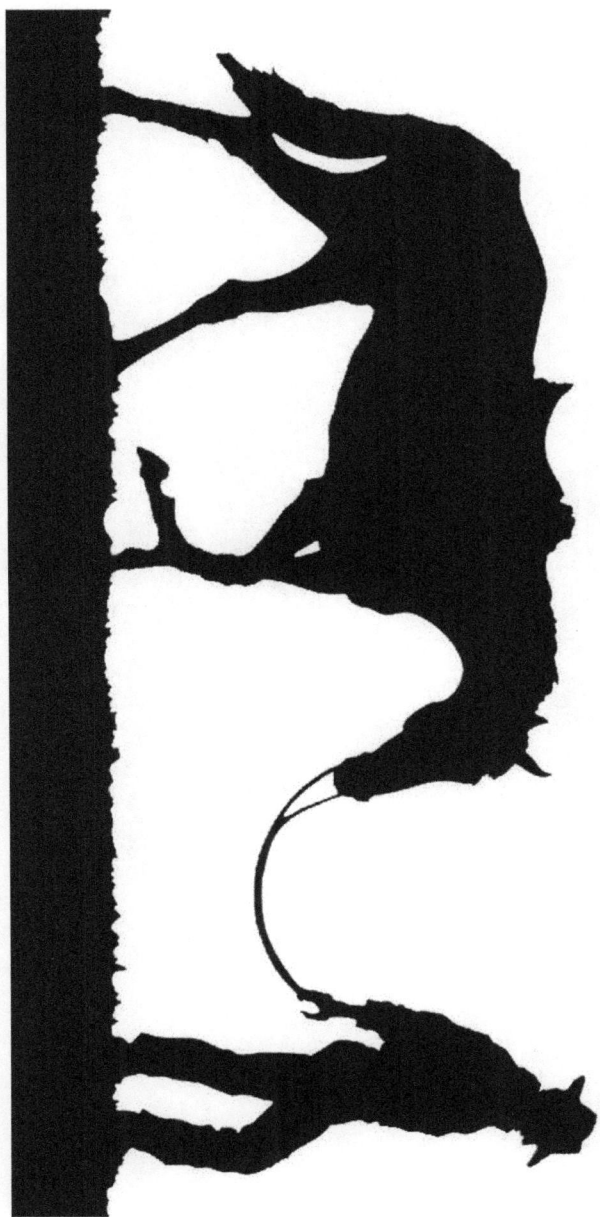

Acknowledgements

I sincerely thank Andy McDermott and his team at Publicious Book Publishing, and Julie Guthrie who transposed my words into type. Thank you for turning this book into truth.